MW00876695

T-SHIRT QUILTING F(

A comprehensive step by step guide to learn the skills and techniques to making beautiful t-shirt quilt patterns from home

Anna Franklin

Table of contents

CHAPTER ONE

Introduction

T-shirt quilting is a well-liked and satisfying hobby that results in a warm, one-of-a-kind souvenir made from one's most treasured T-shirts. T-shirts are cut into squares or rectangles, a pattern is designed, the pieces are sewn together, backing, batting, and quilting are added, and binding is added to complete the quilt. Making a quilt out of old T-shirts is a wonderful way to display cherished keepsakes, express one's individuality, and make something really one-of-a-kind. This outline will take you through the process of making a quilt out of T-shirts and provide advice and ideas along the way.

What is T-shirt quilting

Making a quilt out of used T-shirts is called "T-shirt quilting." T-shirts are cut into squares or rectangles, fusible interfacing is added for stability, and the pieces are sewed together to form a patchwork pattern. Because the T-shirts used often reflect unique events, groups, or hobbies, the finished quilt is not only useful but also functions as a customized memory keeper. Whether they have emotional significance or not, old T-shirts may be put to good use by quilting them into something new and interesting. The finished item may be utilized in a variety of ways, such as a warm and one-of-a-kind blanket, a beautiful wall hanging, or a thoughtful present for someone special.

Benefits of making T-shirt quilts

Making a quilt out of used T-shirts has several advantages.

1. Using your favorite T-shirts to create a patchwork that is both practical and uniquely yours is a great way to keep your memories close at hand for years to come.

2. T-shirt quilting is a fantastic method to give new life to outgrown T-shirts that formerly had special meaning.

3. Personalization: Each T-shirt quilt may be made to suit the maker's taste, hobbies, and life experiences.

4. T-shirt quilting is an environmentally responsible activity since it encourages reusing materials that would otherwise be thrown away.

5. T-shirt quilts are multipurpose, serving as a soft blanket or throw that may be used for both decoration and warmth.

6. Artistic Expression: T-shirt quilting is a fun way to put your artistic skills to use and explore new pattern possibilities.

Making T-shirt quilts is a great way to give old clothes new life while also keeping precious memories close and giving free rein to one's imagination.

Brief history of T-shirt quilting

T-shirt quilting has been around since the '60s and '70s, when the T-shirt was at the height of its popularity as a means of youth expression. different phrases, logos, and images representing different causes, groups, and interests were often printed on T-shirts. Some quilters in the late 1970s and early 1980s started using T-shirts as a means to memorialize loved ones and make their quilts more one-of-a-kind.

T-shirt quilting gained popularity in the 1990s, and many quilters started to focus exclusively on this technique. T-shirt quilting gained popularity as people looked for creative ways to preserve their favorite shirts, particularly those acquired at concerts, sporting events, and other memorable occasions.

T-shirt quilting is still widely practiced, and many quilters now offer their talents in this area of expertise. Because of the proliferation of internet shopping and social media, anybody may now make their own one-of-a-kind T-shirt quilt to save and treasure for years to come.

Choosing T-shirts for quilting

The first step in making a great T-shirt quilt is selecting the appropriate shirts. Here are some suggestions for picking out the right T-shirts for your quilt:

1. Pick T-shirts with meaning: Shirts from significant events or groups that you've been a part of may give a lot of depth to your T-shirt patchwork.

2. Choose T-shirts produced from high-quality fabric that will last a long time. T-shirts that are too thin, too stretched, or too worn may not last long in the quilt.

3. Choose T-shirts with eye-catching designs; for example, you may make a

patchwork out of T-shirts with unique images, logos, and phrases.

4. Think about the palette you want to use for the quilt and choose T-shirts that complement that color scheme.

5. The size of the T-shirts and how they will fit into the quilt pattern are also important factors to think about. T-shirts of a smaller size may be used as building blocks or merged with other T-shirts.

6. have spares: In case some shirts don't fit or you need more to finish your design, you should have some spare T-shirts on hand.

Selecting the appropriate T-shirts is crucial to the end result of your T-shirt patchwork project. Pick T-shirts carefully so that they have significance for you, are long-lasting, intriguing, the proper size, and suit your color scheme and theme.

CHAPTER TWO

Cutting T-shirts into squares or rectangles

T-shirts may be cut into squares or rectangles after they have been picked, washed, and dried. How to properly cut a T-shirt:

1. The greatest instrument for cutting T-shirts is a rotary cutter since it produces crisp, straight lines. Use a blade that is in good working order.

2. Make a template by cutting a square or rectangle to the desired size. All the T-shirt parts will be the same size if you do this.

3. Since the front and back of a T-shirt are not always completely aligned, it's best to cut them out separately. Your T-shirt parts will be more likely to be of the same size if you do this.

4. If you're using a T-shirt with a huge design, you may make a statement with your quilt by cutting around the image. You may alternatively just cut out the pattern using a smaller template and glue it onto a bigger square.

5. If your T-shirts are thin or elastic, you may want to use a stabilizer to keep the shape of your designs intact while you cut and sew.

6. Make sure you have enough materials by cutting extras in case you need to fix a mistake or add something to your design.

An essential part of making a T-shirt quilt is cutting the shirts into squares or rectangles. To guarantee a good and consistent design, it's recommended to use a rotary cutter, make a template, cut the front and back separately, cut around the pattern, apply a stabilizer if required, and cut additional pieces.

Stabilizing T-shirts with fusible interfacing

One common method for making T-shirt quilts involves stabilizing the shirts using fusible interfacing. Instructions for using fusible interfacing to strengthen T-shirts are as follows:

1. T-shirt weight and stretchiness will determine the kind of fusible interfacing you should use. For most T-shirt materials, a thin interfacing works well.

2. Remove any dirt or residue from the T-shirts by washing and drying them before applying the interfacing.

3. Minimize waste by cutting the interfacing to the same dimensions as the T-shirt components, or just a little smaller.

4. Attach the interfacing to the T-shirts by ironing it on, adhesive side down, after positioning it on the back of the garment.

Apply interfacing to the T-shirt by pressing hard with a hot iron for several seconds. All of the T-shirts should be treated in the same way.

5. Using a rotary cutter and a ruler, cut the T-shirts into squares or rectangles after you've applied the interfacing.

6. To prevent the interfacing from adhering to the iron when pressing the T-shirts after application, use a pressing cloth.

If you want a more robust and long-lasting T-shirt quilt, stabilizing the shirts using fusible interfacing before you sew them together is a good idea. To get the best results, choose the correct interface and do all steps exactly as described.

Choosing a layout

The first step in making a T-shirt quilt is deciding on a design. If you're having trouble deciding on a design for your T-shirt quilt, consider these suggestions.

1. Think about the size and form of the T-shirt bits and bobs: the size and shape of the T-shirt bits and bobs you end up with will depend on how you cut the shirts. Think about how you'd want to lay up the components to make a unified whole.

2. Create a plan for the overall look and feel of your T-shirt quilt. Which of symmetry, randomness, or highlighting certain T-shirts or designs do you prefer?

3. In order to better envision your plan, use a design wall. Arrange your T-shirt pieces on a big piece of flannel or felt. You may rearrange the parts without much trouble until you discover a design you like.

4. Maintain a sense of visual harmony by spreading your T-shirt quilt's various colors and patterns out evenly. To get a unified

look, you may want to think about selecting neutral or complimentary materials.

5. You may give your T-shirt quilt a more polished appearance by adding sashing or borders between the individual squares of fabric. You may create visual depth and intrigue by using a solid hue or complementary cloth.

6. Don't be hesitant to try out a few various layouts before settling on one you like. To help you determine which design is best, photograph each possible arrangement.

Choose a layout that best highlights your T-shirt parts by thinking about their size and form, the overall design, balancing the colors and patterns, adding sashing or borders, and playing around with alternative layouts.

Adding sashing or borders

To make your T-shirt quilt seem more put together, try using sashing or borders to frame the individual T-shirt blocks. Some suggestions for bordering or slashing:

1. Select a fabric whose colors and patterns go well with those of your T-shirt parts. Think about utilizing a consistent color scheme or a pattern that complements the whole.

2. Determine the size of the sashing or border strips by measuring the width and length of the T-shirt pieces.

3. Sashing and border strips should be trimmed down to size. A rotary cutter and ruler will allow you to make clean, accurate cuts.

4. Join the strips by stitching them together to make lengthy sashing or border strips. Flatten the seams by pressing them open.

5. Use a quarter-inch seam allowance for sewing the sashing or border strips onto the T-shirt sections. T-shirt parts, sashing, and

borders should all fit together without gaps or misalignment.

6. To achieve a tidy and level surface, push the seams towards the sashing or borders once they have been attached.

7. To give the sashing or border strips more visual weight and depth, cornerstones may be added. The sashing or border strips have cornerstones, which are little squares of cloth sewed into the corners.

You may give your T-shirt quilt a more professional appearance by adding sashing or borders around the individual T-shirt blocks. A T-shirt quilt may be made by selecting a complementing fabric, measuring and cutting strips, sewing them together, connecting them to the T-shirt pieces, stitching the seams, pressing the seams, and adding cornerstones.

CHAPTER THREE

Selecting backing fabric and batting

The success of your T-shirt quilt relies heavily on your choice of background fabric and batting. To assist you in making the most appropriate choices for your quilt, here are some hints:

1. Fabric for the back of the quilt should be strong and long-wearing since it will be the quilt's foundation. Think of utilizing a basic pattern or a plain color to go with the T-shirt styles. Make sure the fabric you chose is broad enough to cover the quilt top and has some extra on each side for the seams.

2. Warmth and loft are provided by the batting, which is located in the quilt's central layer. Pick a cotton or cotton/polyester mix batting, since these are good choices for a T-shirt quilt. Pick batting that will fit snuggly between the backing and the quilt top.

3. Both the background fabric and the batting should be washed and shrunk before being used in the quilt. This helps ensure the finished quilt won't become too small or warp too much.

4. Quilts are layered once the background fabric and batting have been selected. Spread the batting out on a broad, flat area, then lay the backing fabric on top, right sides together. Remove any creases and lumps from the batting. The T-shirt quilt top is then flipped right-side up and placed on top of the batting.

5. To keep the layers from shifting during quilting, baste them together. Baste the layers together with safety pins or spray glue.

You can make a high-quality T-shirt quilt that will endure for years by choosing a robust background fabric and an appropriate batting, washing and pre-shrinking the fabrics, layering the quilt, and basting the layers together.

Sewing T-shirt squares/rectangles together

After deciding on a design, stabilizing the T-shirts, and picking a background fabric and batting, the next step in making a T-shirt quilt is to sew the squares or rectangles together. Here are the directions for assembling the T-shirt shapes:

1. Prepare your work area by laying out the T-shirt components in the proper arrangement. Check that every component has the same orientation before proceeding.

2. To complete the first row of sewing, align the right sides of the top two T-shirt pieces and pin them together. Place them right side together and pin the edge you'll be sewing, leaving a 1/4-inch gap between them. Use a straight stitch to sew along the pinned edge.

3. Repeat this process to join the next row of T-shirt pieces using a 1/4-inch seam allowance. For the next row of T-shirt components, follow the same steps.

4. As soon as you've completed one row of T-shirt components, you may go on to the next. Put right sides together the first two rows. Place them right side together and pin the edge you'll be sewing, leaving a 1/4-inch gap between them. Use a straight stitch to sew along the pinned edge. Sew together each row in this manner until all rows have been completed.

5. Iron the seams: Once the T-shirt components have been sewn together, the seams should be ironed. This process of setting the seams results in a more polished final product.

T-shirt quilt tops may be produced by following these instructions and assembling T-shirt squares or rectangles. The T-shirt quilt is done when the quilt top is layered with batting and backing fabric and quilted.

Sewing sashing and borders

The addition of sashing and borders to a T-shirt quilt may really set it off. How to add borders and sashing to a T-shirt quilt:

1. Sashing and border fabric should be cut to the exact dimensions of your T-shirt quilt top in both length and breadth. It's up to you to decide how big your sashing and border strips should be, but they're usually anywhere from 2 to 4 inches.

2. Attach the sashing by sewing the first sashing strip to the border of the T-shirt quilt top, right sides together. Leave a 1/4-inch gap and pin it in place. Sashing strips are straight-stitched onto the quilt top. Sashing is achieved by placing strips of fabric next to one another and cutting tiny gaps in between them.

3. To attach the border to the T-shirt quilt top, line up the right sides of the first border strip with the edge of the quilt top and sew the two layers together. Leave a 1/4-inch gap and pin it in place. Use a straight stitch to attach the border strip to the quilt top. Use the remaining border strips in the same manner.

4. Once the sashing and borders have been stitched onto the T-shirt quilt top, it is time to press the seams. This process of setting the seams results in a more polished final product.

5. After the top of the T-shirt quilt is finished (sashing, borders, etc.), it is time to add the batting and backing.

6. Tie the layers of your T-shirt quilt together using quilting stitches. Quilting may be done in whatever style you choose, from straight lines to free-motion quilting.

Adding sashing and borders to your T-shirt quilt can help you produce a final product that is both practical and aesthetically pleasing.

Pressing and trimming the quilt top

It's vital to press and trim the T-shirt quilt top once you've done sewing it together and added the sashing and borders. Follow these directions to press and finish the quilt top made from T-shirts:

First, press the T-shirt quilt top with an iron, being sure to focus on the seams, sashing, and borders. All of the seams should be pressed in the same direction, and the sashing and border strips should be pressed toward the quilt's borders.

Second, cut the T-shirt quilt top to size using a rotary cutter, a ruler, and a cutting mat. Straighten and square off the quilt top's edges to the correct dimensions you've set.

Cutting the batting and backing fabric to size, with a few inches added on both sides for quilting and binding, is step three in preparing the quilt top.

The following instructions will help you get your T-shirt quilt top ready for quilting by pressing it, trimming it, and layering it with batting and backing fabric.

Choosing a quilting method

The final appearance and feel of your T-shirt quilt will determine the quilting technique you choose. Here are some potential paths to take:

First, there's the time-honored technique of hand quilting, which is using a needle and thread to sew the quilt layers together. Hand quilting a T-shirt quilt adds a gorgeous, unique touch, but it takes time and practice to perfect.

Machine quilting is a more time- and labor-saving alternative to hand stitching a T-shirt quilt. Machine quilting may be done in a variety of styles, such as free-motion quilting, straight lines, or stippling. A sewing machine and some time spent practicing are all that's needed to add texture and visual interest to a T-shirt quilt made from scraps.

Third, a T-shirt quilt is tied by tying the layers together at regular intervals with knots tied in yarn or embroidery thread. This quilting technique is great for novices or for people who prefer a more relaxed appearance for their T-shirt quilt.

You should choose a quilting technique for your T-shirt quilt based on your own preferences, your degree of expertise, and the appearance and feel you want to accomplish.

CHAPTER FOUR

Preparing the quilt for quilting

It's time to get your T-shirt quilt ready for quilting after you've decided on a quilting technique and completed the top. These are the measures to take:

First, layer the quilt by placing the background fabric face down on a clean, level surface. Remove any creases or folds. Batting goes on top of the background fabric, and the T-shirt quilt top goes on top of that, right side out. Remove any creases or folds from the T-shirt quilt top.

The next step is to baste the layers of the quilt together, which will serve to hold them in place while the quilt is being worked on. The layers may be held together with either safety pins or basting spray. To remove wrinkles and folds from a quilt, begin at the quilt's center and go outward.

Third, if you want to machine quilt the T-shirt quilt top, you should draw the quilting lines. You may use chalk or a fabric pen with water-soluble or disappearing ink to draw the lines.

Quilt the layers together using your preferred quilting technique. If you're using a machine quilting method, stitch along the lines you've drawn. Once you're done quilting, you should bind the quilt or use some other method to fasten the edges.

These guidelines will help you get your T-shirt quilt ready for quilting by hand, machine, or by tying.

Putting the pieces together by quilting

By stitching the quilt top, batting, and backing fabric together, you can construct a sturdy and attractive T-shirt quilt. These are the measures to take:

First, decide on a technique for quilting: To finish your T-shirt quilt, you may either hand quilt it, machine quilt it, or knot it.

Center yourself first: Quilting should start in the middle of the quilt and go outward. The layers are less likely to pucker or bunch up as a result.

Third, make sure you're using the right needle and thread for your project. Machine quilting requires a certain kind of quilting needle and thread.

To replicate the quilting pattern, When quilting, it's important to stay inside the lines of the design, whether you're using a premade pattern or making your own.

5. Take time off: It's important to give your hands and eyes a vacation from quilting every so often.

After you are done quilting, you should bind the quilt or use some other finishing method to secure the edges.

Following these instructions will help you create a T-shirt quilt that is both beautiful and practical, and will be treasured for years to come.

Trimming the quilt and preparing for binding

Quilting a T-shirt top is just half the battle; the other half is trimming and binding. These are the measures to take:

First, remove the surplus batting and backing by cutting it with a rotary cutter and ruler and placing it in a waste basket. Take care to uniformly trim the edges.

To square the quilt, measure and mark the quilt's center at each of the four corners using the ruler. Use the marks on the ruler to draw a line connecting them. Trim along the marked line with the rotary cutter, paying special attention to creating square corners.

To make the binding, first you need to cut strips of cloth. The strips may be cut to whatever width you choose, although 2 1/2 inches is typical. Join the ends of the binding strips with a seam to make one continuous piece. Binding wrong sides together and press in half lengthwise.

Fourth, attach the binding by sewing it to the quilt's edges using a quarter-inch seam allowance, starting on one side and leaving a 6-inch tail. When you get to a corner, fold the binding up at a 45-degree angle and stop sewing 14 inch from the edge of the quilt. After that, you may stitch the binding to the next side by folding it back over the top of the angle. Stop stitching when you reach the beginning and leave a 6-inch tail of binding.

To complete the binding, fold the ends inside to produce a neat finish at the beginning and end. Join the two ends with a stitch and cut off the excess. The binding should be hand stitched to the back of the quilt.

Trimming your T-shirt quilt and getting it ready for binding is a breeze if you follow these instructions. Your T-shirt quilt will be done and ready to use or give as a gift after the binding has been added.

CHAPTER FIVE

Choosing a binding fabric

Selecting an appropriate binding fabric for your T-shirt quilt will complete the quilt and give it a finished appearance. Some advice on how to choose binding fabric:

Think about the color first: If you're making a quilt out of old T-shirts, your choice of fabric should reflect that. Choose a shade that either stands out against the T-shirts or blends in with the crowd.

The second consideration is the quilt's design: if the top has many different designs or prints, the binding cloth should be a solid color. An alternative is to use a binding fabric with a pattern or design if your quilt top is largely solid-colored T-shirts.

Third, consider the size of the print or solid color you'd want to use for the binding if your T-shirts have significant images or patterns. If your T-shirts have modest graphics, however, a larger-scale print on the binding cloth may work better.

Think about the weight: you'll want to choose a fabric that's about the same heft as the T-shirts and backing. The binding's drape and flatness might be affected if the fabric is noticeably heavier or lighter than the rest of the garment.

Try trying a few different fabrics by laying them down next to the quilt top to see which one you like best. If you want to see how the binding fabric looks with the T-shirts, you may use a sample.

You may select a binding fabric that goes well with your T-shirt quilt if you keep these things in mind.

Preparing the binding strips

The procedure for making binding strips for a T-shirt quilt is as follows:

First, measure the dimensions: To accommodate for overlap and corners, add 12 inches to the perimeter measurement of your quilt top. The total length of binding required will be this much. The typical width is 2.5 inches, but you may make it whatever size you choose.

Second, cut the binding fabric into strips of the required width and length using a rotary cutter and ruler. If the length of the strips is insufficient, you may join them end-to-end to make a longer one.

Strips may be joined by placing two strips right sides together at a 90-degree angle and sewing across from corner to corner on the diagonal. Remove the surplus material and push open the seam. Iterate until you get one long, uninterrupted strip, then stop.

After that, you'll need to press the binding strips by folding them in half lengthwise, wrong sides together, and ironing to set the crease. Make sure there is a clean crease and uniform edges.

Now that you've made your binding strips, you can finish off your T-shirt quilt by sewing them on.

Attaching the binding to the quilt

The binding on your T-shirt quilt may be attached in the following ways:

To begin, find the center of one side. Start pinning the binding to the right side of the quilt top, matching the raw edges of the binding with the raw edges of the quilt, leaving approximately 6-8 inches of the binding strip unsewn. Begin at the quilt's centre, and leave a long tail of binding on one side.

Second, attach the binding by sewing it to the quilt with a 1/4-inch seam allowance using a sewing machine. Weave in our thread ends, backstitch, and then take the quilt out of the machine 1/4 inch from the corner.

The next step is to miter the corners, which is done by folding the binding up and away from the quilt top to make a 45-degree angle. The binding is refolded with its raw edges even with the next quilt side. Sew along the next side once you've pinned the corner in place. Do the same thing at each of the four corners.

When you go back to the place where you began stitching the binding, stop approximately 6-8 inches away from the beginning. Reduce the binding length such that it just overlaps the beginning. Overlap the ends of the binding and stitch a straight seam to join them. The quilt's binding must be finished sewn on.

The binding is finished when it is folded over the quilt's raw edge, pinned in place, and pressed. Create a clean crease in the binding by pressing it with an iron.

To complete the binding, step six is to blind stitch or ladder stitch the folded edge of the binding to the back of the quilt. Stitching should be tiny and well-concealed inside the seam allowance.

Following these instructions will help you attach the binding to your T-shirt quilt, giving it a polished, completed look.

Finishing the binding

Finish your T-shirt quilt by doing the following after you've connected the binding:

First, you'll need scissors to remove the bulk from the quilt's corners without slicing through the binding or the top.

Second, fold the binding over so that the folded edge is on the back of the quilt. The binding has to go over the quilt top and cover the seam allowance. The binding may be kept in place using pins.

Blind stitch or ladder stitch the folded edge of the binding to the back of the quilt using a needle and thread for step three of the binding process. Stitching should be tiny and well-concealed inside the seam allowance. The stitching should begin and terminate in a corner.

Fold the binding at a 45-degree angle, and then fold it over itself to make a mitered corner; this completes step 4. Keep sewing after placing pins.

5. Finish the binding by stitching all four sides, then cutting off the excess and tying off the thread. You may now call your T-shirt quilt complete.

Putting on the binding might be a tedious process, but the end result is a quilt that looks finished and professional. Take pleasure in the sentimental value of your new T-shirt quilt.

CHAPTER SIX

Guide to making a T-Shirt Baby Quilt

Since I am not a sewer and this is not going to be an article that explains how to stitch a quilt, I feel the need to be completely forthright right off the bat. If, on the other hand, you are someone who, like me, has been hoarding some old t-shirts and has been looking for a way to put those shirts to good use, then you should definitely adopt this suggestion! Check out the way I was able to reuse years' worth of (mainly free) clothes in order to make a t-shirt baby blanket that is unique to the recipient.

I had a large box full of outgrown t-shirts that I no longer wore, and I stated that I had this box before. You know how sometimes when you attend events or participate in sports teams, you receive free cotton shirts to wear? I used them for a while as pajamas or exercise shirts, but finally I put them all aside since I knew I would be utilizing them for some kind of sewing project in the future. Well, that's what happened.

Now, the very first thing that I did was search for somebody who was capable of making a quilt for me. I was aware that I had a large number of t-shirts and that I intended to construct a quilt of a standard or adult size, but after seeing the picture below, I felt as if I also need a baby blanket.

I mean, those colors are quite stunning, aren't they?

After many months of looking, I was finally successful in locating a person that specialized in making baby blankets! I showed the picture that served as our inspiration, and we came to a consensus on the patch sizes, overall measurements, etc.

After that, I was required to report for duty! After putting together all of my shirts, I began cutting them into pieces. Because I still want to make an adult quilt at some point, I made sure to retain all of the huge patterns for that project.

I used a little square template made of cardboard, and I would cut out as many squares of cloth as I could from each shirt. I used the squares to make a quilt. After some time, I had significant discomfort in my hand, and it took me many days of intermittent labor to complete everything.

When I came across a little design that was the right size for my square, I would cut it out and place it in a separate pile. This would happen whenever I came across it.

When it was all said and done, and all of the shirts had been hacked to shreds, I was left with a variety of colors... and also a great collection of rags. Score!

I believe that this is when the magic started to happen. I have arranged for all of my patchwork squares to be assembled into a quilt and have sent them out. It took me days to cut up all of those t-shirts into squares, and my squares weren't even very straight. I'm not going to lie to you guys about that. What quilters have to go through to create the ideal designs is beyond my ability to fathom... despite this, it is a skill, and their hands are probably made of steel!

Finally, I was able to get my hands on the completed baby quilt made from my old t-shirts, and I couldn't be happier with it!

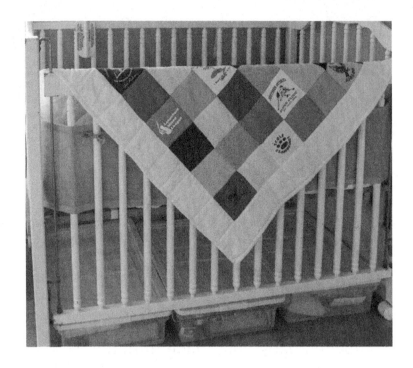

Even though the design was based on the picture that served as inspiration, the addition of all of the minor graphics really helped to differentiate it and make it seem more personalized to me.

In addition, I am aware that we are now in the midst of summer, but despite the fact that winter is still a ways off, this quilt could come in handy for us.

Or, you could simply put it on display and not worry about it being damaged in any way!

At the moment, the personalized t-shirt baby quilt is folded up neatly and stored in the baby's cot in the nursery. Because the baby does not yet take up a significant amount of room in the crib, we also store our other blankets there. I can't wait till he's older so I can explain the meaning behind all of the pictures that are on his quilt:)

One of these days, I'll get around to learning how to sew or commissioning someone else to make a giant quilt out of the remaining pieces of my old t-shirts. I'm not sure which will come first, lol! But until then, I have a wonderful quilt, and I'm extremely glad that I was able to recycle materials that have emotional meaning to me (plus they take up less room this way!). But until then, I have a wonderful quilt.

start all of your materials together, and then start to work.

CHAPTER SEVEN

STEP BY STEP GUIDE TO QUILTING A SIMPLE T-SHIRT

Learn how to construct a very simple T-shirt quilt with no batting, no sashing between the shirts, a microfleece (or other fabric) backing, and no binding. This quilt may be made with whatever fabric you choose for the backing.

STEPS TO FOLLOW:
1. Obtain all of the Necessary Items

o Sewing Machine with a Baby Lock

o T-shirts

o Lightweight Fusible Interfacing (I always get a half yard per t-shirt)

o Backing (we'll discuss how much in step 9)
o Lightweight Fusible Interfacing (I always get a half yard each t-shirt)

o Thread

2. To get started, you will need to choose the size of the quilt you want to make as well as its proportions.

A chart with the approximate final measurements may be seen below. If you have nine squares, you should create shirts that are three squares by three squares (this will result in a rather tiny lap quilt, and this could be the place where you want to add sashing). Check out the instruction that is located here. If you have 12 shirts, you may divide them into three rows of four or four rows of three. 16 shirts equals four sets of four, 24 shirts equals four sets of six, 25 shirts equals five sets of five, and so on. I find it helpful to sketch up a diagram since I am very visual, and it enables me to calculate how much support I will need.

I. Size Guide for the T-Shirt Quilt

Title of Quilt | Approximate Size | Estimated Number of T-Shirts

☐ Lap | 45" x 45" | 9 or 12...

☐ Large Lap | 45" x 60" |12 or 16...

Twin: 60" x 90" (long twin) or 75" x 75" (standard twin) | 16, 20, 24, 25...

Wide Full | 75" x 90" or 90" x 90" (standard full) | 20, 25, 30, 36...

☐ Queen | 90" x 105" | 25, 30, 36, 42...

☐ Measure both the smallest and largest graphic shirts after selecting the King size shirt which is 105 inches by 105 inches and the sequence of shirt sizes starting from 30 and increasing by 6 (i.e., 36, 42, 49, 56, etc.).

This will define the size of each square; if you have particularly huge pictures, you may need to sacrifice part of some of them in order to accommodate this. A decent size is 15 inches by 15 inches or 16 inches by 16 inches...Keep in mind that the finished square will be 1/2 inch shorter on each side due to the half-inch seam allowance that was used. You have the choice of making the squares larger or smaller. For instance, if you have a lot of t-shirts, you may make the squares smaller so that the quilt doesn't end up being too large. The quilt in the example consists of 25 squares and has a completed dimension of 75 inches by 75 inches (each square was cut at 16 inches by 16 inches, which resulted in their being sewed to 15 inches by 15 inches).

It's time to start cutting now that you have your dimensions in hand.

If you are going to use both sides of the shirt, use the scissors to cut the sides as equally as possible up the sides of the shirt, making sure that you will have enough to cut your desired dimensions out of it (if you need to add more fabric to any of the pieces to make them the correct size, check out this guide). If you are just going to use one of the sides, you simply need to trim the back. Cut off a portion of your sleeve, but not all of it, since you may need part of it in order to maintain the square shape of your cut across the width of the sleeve. After that, cut an opening in the shoulder seam. If you cut the back, you may then trim the sides a little so that you don't have too much surplus material (see an image of a shirt that has been cut for an example). .

I. To attach the facings to each shirt: For each shirt, cut a piece of interfacing about half a yard.

When ironing your cut shirt, take cautious not to stretch it and press it with the front facing down. The next step is to begin at the top of your shirt by placing a piece of interfacing on it and positioning it so that it is as straight and centered as you can make it. Begin from the top and work your way down, being sure to use a cover cloth since this lightweight interfacing has a tendency to cling to the iron if one is not used. This will help to stabilize your shirt quite a bit, which will make it much easier to cut it evenly and accurately. Take your time so that the ingredients can properly combine. (It should be noted that not all t-shirt quilters use interfacing; those who do like the fact that the shirt has some give to it and is less heavy overall. Stability and precision are two qualities that appeal to me about it.

When you are through with the interface, you may go on to cutting your squares.

My preference is to cut even squares since it makes it easier for me to avoid making mistakes. However, if you have some lengthy designs and you would want to cut rectangles, you absolutely may do so; the only thing you need to keep in mind is to remember your measures each time you go to cut. You can use a square ruler and scissors instead of a rotary cutter (draw your lines and cut them...you could even develop a pattern or cut your first one extremely well and use it as a pattern), but I prefer a rotary cutter since it gives me greater precision. When using a rotary cutter, you should first lay out your shirt on the mat and visually inspect it or use a ruler to ensure that it is straight. The majority of designs are closer to the top, therefore you want as much room above the image as possible so that it appears more even above and below. For most t-shirts, cut initially as closely as possible to the top edge (the neckline). After you have finished cutting the top, measure how far down you need to cut and then begin cutting. Next, you'll need to trim your sides. I usually start with a large cut and work my way inside to ensure that the image is centered on the shirt (t-shirt graphics aren't always entirely centered or even; for this reason, I try to eyeball it more than measure it, and thus far, this strategy has worked)! For the sake of precision, whenever I cut anything, I measure, re-measure, and measure once again...It would be a shame to cut it an inch too short. You want to make sure that your cuts are as equal and exact as they can be so that you can stitch and line up your seams accurately when you sew your rows together!

To begin from the very beginning

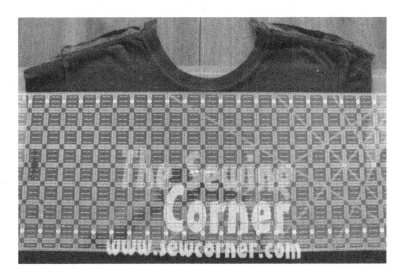

I. Get the cut as near as you can to the neckline! First remove the bottom, then the sides (while attempting to preserve the image in the middle, if that is what is intended).

Put your t-shirts on the floor so you may evaluate several ways to arrange them. It's important to me that the colors are well distributed and that the overall effect is as pleasing to the eye as it can be.

Now that your squares are all cut out, it's time to start sewing them into rows!

It makes no difference which row you start with; nevertheless, I find it easiest to work my way down from the top row. Make sure you are sewing the correct seam for the correct order of your shirts...it's always a bummer to sew the incorrect side when you open up the shirts or something is upside down...double checking before you sew isn't a bad idea. For your first row, lay #1 square on #2 square (pretty sides together) and

sew the left side (each seam is sewn at a 12"
or make use of the foot with needle at the far
left). The key to creating an even and precise
quilt is consistency. There are occasions
when the interface has a tendency to drag on
the foot...You may either attempt to push it
through a little bit further, reduce the
amount of pressure used by the presser foot
(for instructions on how to do this, see the
handbook for your machine), or use a
walking foot instead. Next, you will place #3
on #2 and stitch the right edge, and then
you will continue in this manner (#4 on #3
and sew the right edge, #5 on #4 and sew
the right edge). When you've completed one
row, go on to the next row and repeat the
process. To reduce the bulk, I prefer to press
my seam allowances open while sewing rows
together. Although I haven't faced any
trouble in aligning my rows this way, I
suggest being cautious while ironing if

there's any graphic visible in the seam allowance, by using a cover cloth.

When sewing rows together, some individuals prefer to press both seam allowances in one direction to create a ridge that helps in aligning the seams. If you choose to follow this method, iron the seam allowances in the same direction for one row and then in the opposite direction for the next row.

First Place on the Second Number Stitch the left seam (found below).

I. Put the number 3 on top of the number 2
and stitch the right seam

II. Put the number 4 on top of the number 3, then stitch the right seam

III. All the squares have been sewed together to produce all the rows!

Now it's time to stitch your rows together!

Pinning my seams equally first (to verify that they are even) and then pinning once or twice inside the square is my preferred method. When I'm sewing, I remove the pins from the fabric before I get to them, but in some situations, like this one, I prefer to leave the pins in for increased efficiency and more stability (I simply stitch more slowly whenever I come close to a pin)...The jersey has a tendency to shift about on you, and this is particularly true if there is a shirt seam in the vicinity. Therefore, you will fold row 1 down into row 2 (with the lovely sides together, as seen in the figure below), pin it, and then sew the top seam (make sure you are sewing the proper location so that you don't have to pull out a whole row of stitches)! Open up the lengthy seam allowance you created by pressing it, using a cover cloth if required. After turning row 3 down onto row 4, pin the top edge, stitch along the pinned edge, and then press the seam open.Below: I pinned my seams to ensure that they were equal (I always pin both sides of my seam allowances before sewing, so that they don't get folded over on themselves!

I. Stitching Row 1 onto Row 2 to create the top seam

Make sure that the shirts are facing the correct direction when you open it so that you do not accidentally sew rows together in the incorrect sequence or anything that is the wrong way around.

II. Join rows 1 and 2 together, then rows 3 and 4, and finally join rows 5 and 6.

I divide it up so that I'm not sewing four rows together to make one, which is a little bit easier to manage now that the quilt is becoming heavier.

III. Join the first and second rows together, then join the third, fourth, and fifth rows.

IV. Sewing the top two rows to the bottom three rows (and pinning the seams and the spaces in between) is the fourth step.

V. The quilt top has been completed; check!

The top of your T-shirt quilt is now complete! Yay! We are going to cut the backing at this point.

In the event that the length of your quilt top is more than the width of the backing fabric (which, in most cases, would be 45" or 60" unless you acquire proper quilt backing fabric), you will be need to sew a seam along the middle of the quilt (as seen by the photo). If you need to sew a seam, measure the width of your quilt, multiply that number by two, and then divide that number by 36 to find out how much yardage you need (I prefer to place my seam halfway down the quilt back rather than along the center of the blanket from top to bottom... maybe that makes sense (see the photo below)). I sewed it using microfleece...It is really hospitable and warm, but you can make it out of anything soft...fleece, flannel, ordinary cotton...After you have finished stitching the seam, lay the backing out with the seam facing down and the lovely side facing up. Then, with the right sides of your quilt top and backing together, lay your quilt top with the lovely side down. Now you will want to cut your back with your front (NOTE: The picture below shows cutting exactly even, but I would cut an inch or two bigger around the whole edge to avoid fabric shrinkage). Now that you have your back and front cut, you can go on to the next step. Next, pin your quilt all the way around (I like to double pin an area, noting where I start sewing and where I stop to make sure that I remember to leave a large enough hole (the width of a t-shirt) to turn the quilt right side out) (I like to double pin an area to make sure that I remember to leave a big enough hole (the width of a t-shirt) to turn the quilt right side out). After the quilt has been pinned, begin sewing from one double pin and working your way around the whole quilt, stopping when you reach the second double pin and backstitching at the beginning and end of each section. Remove your four corners, then flip your project inside out through the hole you created.Pictured here is: The backing will have a seam through the centre of it.

If you are using microfleece or anything else that has a nap, you need to ensure that the nap faces the same direction when the fabric is opened back up after stitching.

I. The top of the quilt should have the correct sides together and be centered on the quilt backing!

II. Make the backing of your quilt an inch or two larger than the quilt top.

Because of this, you will have some room for error in the event that it contracts, as mine did when I did not leave an additional inch as illustrated above.

III. The whole perimeter of the edge is pinned.

After that, lay the quilt out flat (you may want to push the edge of the quilt a little bit at this point).

Getting it to lie flat and properly may need a little bit of modification on your part (this is particularly true if you are using microfleece or anything similar). Put several pins through both layers in the corners and in the spaces between them all the way around the outside edge. You should try to cover the hole using pins as much as possible (see the figure below for an example), and then stitch around the whole outside edge even with the foot, positioning your needle in the middle (this should be approximately 3/8 inch from the edge). You should make every effort to keep the backing rolled to the back (if you are having problems, you may want to pin it further; the backing could show a little bit if you are using microfleece or anything similar). For the top stitching, I used a gray thread, and for the bobbin, I chose a thread that matched my background cloth. You may find it helpful to switch to a larger stitch as well (3.0 stitch length as compared to 2.5 stitch length).

In the next image, you can see the opening through which the quilt was turned right side out.

I. Closing the hole with pins and folding the edges inward in an even and straight manner as much as feasible.

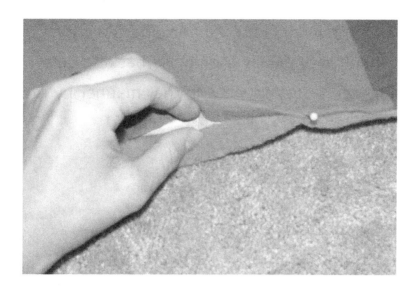

II. The pins have entirely filled up the hole.

III. Stitching all the way around the edge, while continuously sliding the backing below so that it doesn't show in that manner by my thumb.

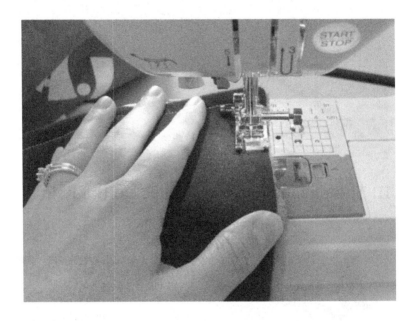

IV. Closing the hole with the needle and thread.

V. Don't let the edge roll like this; instead, keep rolling it under while you stitch to prevent it from showing. Pinning can help hold it under!

During step six, I stitched the full perimeter of the quilt's border by propping it up against the machine's side.

Congratulations, you've made it to the last stage!

Place the quilt back on the floor and stretch it out so that it is level and flat. Stitching the quilt together requires going through both layers of fabric at the corners and along the seams of each shirt. While you stitch, your backing will remain in place thanks to this. Now that your rows and columns are assembled, you will sew or quilt down each seam to secure your backing to your quilt top. This will be done in the same direction as your seams. It's recommended that you begin with the seams in the middle of the blanket and work your way outward; roll the edges of the blanket on each side of the seam that needs to be sewed (see image). Take your time since it is thick and heavy, and the backing may attempt to shift on you. As a result, you will need to pin it many times to guarantee that it remains in place. If you are still experiencing issues, you might try using a walking foot, decreasing the pressure you use to the presser foot, and continuing to utilize the stitch length of 3.0. It is possible that you will still need to assist it by pulling slightly and keeping the front and back taut. Be careful not to pull too hard, as this might cause your needle and/or thread to break; you also don't want your stitches to be too lengthy. In the event that either your needle or your thread breaks, try not to freak out too much since it's not the end of the world! :D This phase is arguably the most challenging since the quilt is normally quite heavy and tough to push through the machine. since of this, you should take your time, but you should also take pauses if you get upset! Make frequent alterations to your quilt so that it may be sewn with more ease.Below: The sides will be rolled around the seam before it is sewed!

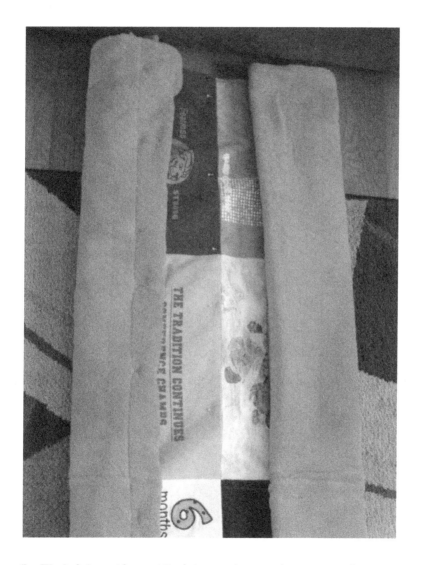

I. Finishing the stitching along the seam!

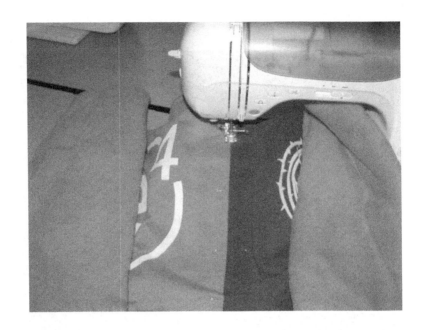

II. You've accomplished everything!!! Thank you so much; I hope you love your new warm blanket! Product in its final form!

Final thoughts on the T-shirt quilting process

T-shirt quilting is an excellent method for preserving memories as well as creating a one-of-a-kind and individualized quilt. The process of sewing a quilt out of old T-shirts might be laborious and time-consuming, but the finished product is always unique and worth the effort. A few concluding remarks on the process of quilting T-shirts are as follows:

• Take care in the selection of your T-shirts: Choose T-shirts for the quilt that either have particular memories for you or have emotional significance for the person who will receive the quilt.

• Prepare in advance: Invest some time in planning out the design and pattern of your quilt, and make use of a design wall so that you can better see the end result.

• Exercise extreme caution while cutting: carefully cut your T-shirts into squares or rectangles, and for maximum accuracy, use a rotary cutter.

• Give some thought to the stabilization of your T-shirts: During the process of quilting, fusible interfacing may be used to assist stabilize your T-shirts and prevent stretching or distortion from occurring.

• Take your time: quilting a T-shirt quilt is a procedure that takes a lot of time, so it's crucial to take your time and have patience during the whole project. It is in your best interest to spend a little more time if doing so will guarantee that your quilt will continue to look excellent for many years to come.

• Experiment with various quilting techniques: Whether you decide to quilt by hand, by machine, or by tying, you should try out a variety of techniques in order to identify the one that works best for you.

• Appreciate the journey: T-shirt quilting is a labor of love, so it is important to take the time to appreciate the journey and the memories that are represented by each T-shirt while you work on your project.

Keeping these pointers in mind will allow you to make a T-shirt quilt that is both lovely and meaningful, and it will be something that will be appreciated for many years to come.

Made in the USA
Coppell, TX
20 November 2024

40617149R00056